We Love Race Cars

by Katherine Lewis

BUMBA BOOKS™

LERNER PUBLICATIONS ◆ MINNEAPOLIS

Note to Educators

Throughout this book, you'll find critical-thinking questions. These can be used to engage young readers in thinking critically about the topic and in using the text and photos to do so.

Lerner Publications Company
An imprint of Lerner Publishing Group, Inc.
241 First Avenue North
Minneapolis, MN 55401 USA

For reading levels and more information, look up this title at www.lernerbooks.com.

Main body text set in Helvetica Textbook Com Roman.
Typeface provided by Linotype AG.

Editor: Brianna Kaiser **Photo Editor:** Brianna Kaiser
Lerner team: Sue Marquis

Library of Congress Cataloging-in-Publication Data

Names: Lewis, Katherine, 1996– author.
Title: We love race cars / Katherine Lewis.
Description: Minneapolis : Lerner Publications, 2021 | Series: Bumba books — we love cars and trucks | Includes bibliographical references and index. | Audience: Ages 4–7 | Audience: Grades K–1 | Summary: "Race cars are made for speed. Readers will zoom through this book to see how race cars are specially designed to move fast and offer peak performance"– Provided by publisher.
Identifiers: LCCN 2020019942 (print) | LCCN 2020019943 (ebook) | ISBN 9781728419275 (library binding) | ISBN 9781728420325 (paperback) | ISBN 9781728419312 (ebook)
Subjects: LCSH: Automobile racing—Juvenile literature. | Sports cars—Juvenile literature.
Classification: LCC GV1029 .L49 2021 (print) | LCC GV1029 (ebook) | DDC 796.72—dc23

LC record available at https://lccn.loc.gov/2020019942
LC ebook record available at https://lccn.loc.gov/2020019943

Manufactured in the United States of America
1-49043-49259-6/16/2020

Table of Contents

Let's Go, Race Cars!

Vroom, vroom! Race cars

zoom around a track.

The fastest one wins!

stock cars

Drivers race many kinds of cars.

Stock cars look like regular cars.

Open-wheel cars are low to the ground.

The driver sits in an open cockpit.

How are stock cars different from open-wheel cars?

Race cars have powerful engines.

Some engines run on gasoline, and

some run partly on electricity.

Most race car engines are very loud.

Race car tires are called slicks.

They don't have grooves.

This helps them grip the road.

Some race cars have spoilers.
Spoilers act like upside-down
airplane wings to push the car
onto the road.
Spoilers help keep fast cars
under control.

spoiler

Race cars drive on tracks. Some tracks are ovals, while others are long, straight lines.

Why do you think cars race on a special track?

Tracks can also wind through

cities or mountains.

Fans love to watch cars

speed to the finish line.

Race cars keep getting

faster and faster!

Parts of a Race Car

spoiler

cockpit

engine

slicks

Picture Glossary

cockpit

the area where a driver sits and controls a race car

open-wheel car

a race car that is low to the ground and has an open cockpit

spoiler

a part of a race car that helps it stay under control

stock car

a race car that looks like a regular car

Learn More

Bach, Rachel. *The Car Race.* Mankato, MN: Amicus Ink, 2017.

Greenwood, Nancy. *I Can Be a Race Car Driver.* New York: Gareth Stevens, 2021.

Reinke, Beth Bence. *Race Cars on the Go.* Minneapolis: Lerner Publications, 2018.

Index

Photo Acknowledgments

Image credits: Sergei Bachlakov/Shutterstock.com, pp. 5, 23 (top right); Grindstone Media Group/Shutterstock.com, pp. 6, 10, 14–15, 18, 20–21, 23 (top left, bottom right); Petr Nad/Shutterstock.com, p. 9; mekcar/Shutterstock.com, pp. 13, 23 (bottom left); Vadim Ivanov/Shutterstock.com, p. 17; Ev. Safronov/Shutterstock.com, p. 22.

Cover: Grindstone Media Group/Shutterstock.com.